TIPS ON TESTING:

STRATEGIES FOR TEST-TAKING

BY

ROBERT L. ALFORD, Ph.D.
Testing Bureau
Norfolk State College
Norfolk, Virginia

This booklet is planned to aid you, the student/
administrator in comprehending and evaluating
the types of tests which are often required of
persons in education. It is the author's hope
that this "Tips on Testing" will encourage a
positive attitude towards test-taking.

TABLE OF CONTENTS

"Test Him! Test Him! Thus Sayeth the Lord"
by R.L. Alford, Ph.D.

Approach the test confidently. Take it calmly.

Remember to review, the week before the test.

Don't "cram." Be careful of your diet and sleep.
..Especially as the time draws nigh.

FOREWORD

Arrive on time. . .and ready.

Choose a good seat. Get comfortable and relax.

Bring the complete kit of "tools" you'll need.

Standardized tests have been used in American schoo
for more than 50 years. They serve many useful purposes
for school administrators, teachers, counselors, parents
and students themselves. The development of tests has
become a complex science. People can easily be confused
the variety of tests, the scoring methods, and the uses
which the results are applied.

This booklet is intended to help you, the student,
understand the kinds of tests that are given to you and
make the most of the test scores for planning your educa
tional progress and setting future goals.

When educators use the word "standardized" they are
talking about a highly specific concept in education.
"Standardized" means that a test is designed so that eve
one who takes it does so under the same conditions: the
same instructions and the same time limits. This ensure
that the results from tests given at different times and
different places can be meaningfully compared. Such
uniformity furnishes a constant point of reference with
which we can compare individual scores and provides a wa
of measuring the student's achievement relative to that
of other students.

Mutually agreed on reference points are necessary t
today's educators. Americans are on the move. Families
often change residences while their children are of scho
age. If there were no agreement on what Grade 2 means f
one school to another, students, teachers, and parents
would be unnecessarily confused. Additionally, some
measure of what skills the student has mastered must be
available to the new school, in a form that can be under
stood without knowing much about the previous teachers o
school system.

Standardized tests are essential within a single
school. They are an important addition to the other
methods available for evaluating a student's progress. T
classroom teacher's evaluation of performance is useful,
because it is concerned with limited content span and lo
goals. Standardized tests add another, objective, measu
of achievement that can be compared with a common criteri

A wide variety of tests are available today. Most f
into one of two broad categories. Some tests measure
academic <u>achievement</u>; others measure what a student has
already learned in a particular area. Others are design
to indicate a student's <u>aptitude</u>; others assess his or h
ability to learn and the likelihood of success in future

2

study.

ACHIEVEMENT TESTS

The tests most often used in educational settings measure academic achievement in reading, English grammar, mathematics, science, and social studies. These tests are two types: <u>norm-referenced</u> tests and <u>criterion-referenced</u> tests. These two types of tests have different purposes and provide different types of information. Both have a place in the educational process.

In a <u>norm-referenced test</u>, the score of each student can be compared with the scores of other students, who have taken the same test under standardized conditions. In this way, it is possible to tell where a student stands in relation to other students in the same grade or group.

Norm-referenced tests, which are widely used today, are developed in a systematic way. Test questions are written, by teachers with several years of classroom experience, to test academic skills that represent current educational curricula. Next, these questions are given to sample groups of students at the appropriate grade levels to find out if the questions measure what they are supposed to measure. Finally, after questions that do not work have been discarded, the entire test is given to a large group that has been carefully chosen to be representative of school children in the United States.

Several kinds of scores have been developed for norm-referenced achievement tests, because no one has been able to invent a single test score that will serve all the purposes for which test scores are used. The three types of scores must frequently encountered are: percentile rank, grade equivalent, and stanine. <u>Percentile Rank</u> reflects a student's performance in comparison with the performance of a specific group of similar students, frequently a cross-section of students in the United States, who are in the same grade and who took the same test at the same time of year. For example, if a student were at the 80th percentile (nationally) when tested near the end of third grade on a reading test, this would mean that he or she scored higher in reading than 80 per cent of all third graders, if they had taken the same test at the same time of year. Percentile ranks range from 1 to 99, with the average rank being 50.

Sometimes local percentile ranks are used. These percentile ranks give comparisons within smaller groups such as among students in one school, district, or state.

3

A grade equivalent relates a student's performance t
the level of performance that is typical for a specific
grade in school. For example, if a student scores 3.5 or
mathematics test, this means the student performed on tha
mathematics test like a typical third grader in the fifth
month of the school year.

When a student's grade equivalent is markedly highe
or lower than the student's grade at the time of testing
the score should be interpreted with considerable cautior
For example, if a second grader scores 5.0 on a mathemat
test that was intended for second grade use, this does no
mean that the student is ready to master fifth-grade math
matics. The student probably has not mastered long division, which is not taught until the fourth grade. In th
case, the score of 5.0 should be interpreted as being fa
superior to the scores achieved by most second graders, t
not as representing the level of attainment in mathemati
typical of a fifth grader.

A stanine is a score that ranges from 1 to 9, with
average performance at 5, with 9 as the highest and 1 as
the lowest scores. A stanine score places a student on
this scale by comparing his or her performance with the
performance of a group of other students. As with the
percentile rank, this comparison group can be made up of
national sample or a smaller local sample. Unless the g
is carefully defined the score will have little meaning.

Criterion-referenced tests measure a student's mast
of the specific objectives of an educational program. N
comparisons are made between students' scores. This kin
of test aids in tailoring each student's learning progra
to his or her own specific needs and talents.

The purpose of criterion-referenced testing is to
determine which specific skills have been mastered and
which have not. For example, on a criterion-referenced
mathematics test, results might indicate "knows how to d
long division. Does not know how to divide fractions," a
so on for each skill taught at the student's learning le
Knowing what objectives a student has not yet learned en
bled the teacher to work more efficiently, by concentratin
on those skills yet to be mastered.

APTITUDE TEST

So far, we have talked about tests that measure a
student's actual achievement: what he or she has learne
Another form of standardized test was developed to measu
aptitude for school learning. Some of these tests are

4

popularly called "IQ tests." IQ stands for intelligence quotient, a form of aptitude score. Publishers usually set the average IQ on their tests at 100. About one-sixth of all students will score above 116, and one-sixth below 84. There are many other measures of a student's ability to learn. An IQ is only a single aptitude score. We should beware of assigning it too much respect. (8:1-6)

Lately, there has been much discussion and controversy surrounding the definition of and use of aptitude tests in education. Although individual opinions vary, it is reasonable not to consider an aptitude score a fixed or permanent measure of a student's potential. Such a score represents an estimate, at the time of testing, of the likelihood of the student's success in future study in areas related to the aptitude being measured. Valuable information has been gained from the practice of comparing a prediction of achievement made from an aptitude test to the student's actual performance on an achievement test.

. Listen carefully to all directions.

. Apportion your time intelligently with an "Exam Budget."

. Read all directions carefully. Twice if necessary.
  Pay particular attention to the scoring plan.

INTRODUCTION

. Look over the whole test before answering any questions.

. Start right in, if possible. Stay with it. Use every
  second effectively.

. Do the easy questions first; postpone harder questions
  until later.

As soon as you select the college of your choice the college will need to know your chances of succeeding in the system of higher education, in fact, oriented to middle-class values. If the school were oriented to another system, then our test would not be culturally biased, but they would be inappropriate.

The basic purpose of scholastic aptitude tests is not to obtain an innate measure of intelligence, but to measure a student's academic potential for acheivement in higher education. Thus the answer to the national charge of cultural bias is, Yes, tests are culturally biased. I have been asked many times to defind the existence of cultural biases in psychological testing. In view of what we all know of American history, my defense states that Minorities in this country have been stigmatized by racism, racism is institutionalized, education is an institution, psychologycal testing is symbiotically related to education and I rest my case, unless it is necessary for me to enter a discourse on the extent to which racism is institutionalized in America. My position is that psychological tests reveal nothing more than a score and under no circumstances should be used as indices of intelligence. Peter Koening writing in Psychology Today accurately assesses that the purpose of psychological testing is "....to measure differences between individuals." Koening also points out that psychological testing has replaced the old credentiality system where in the right family and Ivy League dipolma served as the standard governing over who is going to judge whom.

If I should sound as though I am against testing, let me make it perfectly clear that I do not advocate the total elimination of use of tests as a means of measuring intelligence and the quality of education a person will receive. Yes, we the members of the Testing Bureau at Norfolk State College know that many tests are biased, but for that matter so are the public schools themselves, in favor of White middle America...

Our present testing system needs a great deal of improvement, but this improvement lies in better test construction and use rather than in test elimination. Cultural handicaps will not be remoded by changing tests; only changing the conditions within our society that promote these deprivations will do that. Once you complete your curriculum of study the whole world awaits to test you. Testing for the rest of your life will all happen at an exact time, ready or not it will not await you. A series of tension releasing exercises are recommended to be conducted for approximately fifteen minutes before the beginning of the test. Be ahead of time, be on top of time, never allow time to be on top of you. It' is our hypotheses that any person taking the Freshman Placement Examination will be "doing his/her best". If the conditions of uniformity of testing are to be maintained, every person should be motivated and expected to "do his/her best". The importance of motivation to the examinee's test behavior has been demonstrated in a number of studies Test anxiety and free-floating anxiety are closely related to test-taking motivation. The highly motivated student, for example, may be so anxious to do well that his very deisre may interfere with a good score. The person who is tense makes errors he would not normally commit. The student of measurement knows that there is a great deal of anxiety and tension during testing. Again, do your best and do not prolong your valuable time on an answer you cannot think of, go on to the next test item and return if time permits. Always read the directions carefully for each type of question and be sure that you understand them before you try to answer any questions. Do not worry if you do not have time to finish it. Many of the students who take the test do not attempt all of the questions, and no one is expected to know the answers to all of them. Since you have only a limited amount of time for the test, you should work carefully and as rapidly as possible.

- Determine the pattern of the test questions. If it's hard-easy etc., answer accordingly.

- Read each question carefully. Make sure you understand each one before you answer. Re-read, if necessary.

- Think! Avoid hurried answers. Guess intelligently.

TEST WISENESS

- Watch your watch and "Exam Budget," but do a little balancing of the time you devote to each question.

- Get all the help you can from "cue" words.

- Refresh yourself with a few, well-chosen rest pauses during the test.

Living comfortably with tests, taking them in stride and doing as well as you possibly can on them without the tensions that waste energy, requires a certain basic knowledge of what tests are like.

For comfort in the fact of an approaching test, nothing beats "Knowing your stuff," and knowing that you know it. No amount of "test-wiseness" or inside information or last-minute cramming is a substitute for clear command of the skills and knowledge to be demonstrated on the test-either for the sake of calmness before the test or for the sake of a good score report after it. So the things to know and do listed here are to be considered additional provisions for test comfort after the student has done all he can to develop the learnings which the test will ask him to demonstrate.

HOW TO PREPARE FOR STANDARDIZED TESTS

People preparing to take a test are about as different in their approaches as ball players coming to bat. Some players spit on their hands, some pick up a handful of dirt, some carefully straighten their caps, some shift their chewing gum from right side to left, and some do all of these things. The list of suggestions that teachers-and parents-might make to students who are preparing for a test is not long, but all the suggestions are important.

1. It is sensible to review, if one has time before taking an achievement test, but not blindly. Any test that comes along will cover learnings that have been acquired over an extended period of time, so it will be too late to try to do all the original reading or practice which should have been done. A general review of the main ideas in a course or subject will help to refresh them in the individual's memory.

2. It is useless to cram the night before the test. Last-minute burning of the midnight oil may save a student's scalp with a teacher-made test, but for a standardized test this is worse than no preparation. The standardized test is less devoted to factual information than to skill in using information, so a person's chances of acquiring needed facts in a last-minute cram session are next to nil. Not even professional coaching schools that claim to prepare students for college admissions test can accomplish any significant changes by cramming. There is no late and short

substitute for learning that which should have been
acquired over a long period of time-at least not
in academic subjects. To attempt it is to ask for
other handicaps on the test-fatigue and confusion.

3. Having reviewed sensibly as much as possible in the
   time available, most students are better off to
   relax by doing something different to take their
   minds off the test the afternoon and evening before
   the test comes up. A good night's sleep is a good
   investment.

4. Most important of all, of course, is to encourage
   learning the things at the time and in the sequence
   in which the school teaches them. If a student has
   done this, when any test comes along he is prepared.

HINTS ON TAKING STANDARDIZED TESTS

Some students have a slight advantage over others in
taking tests because they have acquired, through experience or study, a kind of test know-how. Much of this know-
how applies to all standardized tests and resembles, in its
application, the advantage an experienced taxpayer had in
filling out the federal income tax return. The object is
not to cheat, but to avoid unnecessary losses.

Much of what a student needs to do he can do before
he encounters the test fact to fact. In the testing
situation itself, there are things to be done just before
the test starts or while it is being taken.

1. The student must be sure that he understands the
   directions. After he has read the directions
   aloud, the examiner will pause and ask the group
   if anyone has any questions. If any part of what
   is to be done is not crystal-clear, the student
   should raise his hand and ask the question. This
   is why the examiner paused to ask for questions.
   In an important test, it is sheer idiocy to start
   work before all the directions are clearly under-
   stood. And if there is confusion about directions
   in the interior of the test, the examiner or
   proctor will come to the student's seat and help
   interpret the directions.

2. The identification blanks on the answer sheet
   must be filled out exactly as the examiñer directs
   while he is giving these directions. If the student is reading something else while these directions are given, intending to complete these blank
   after he has finished the test, there is a chance
   that he will forget something important.

3. Digging in the way a sprinter does to start a race
   and being prepared to concentrate one's whole
   attention on the test for the whole time that is
   allowed may be hard for people, who are not accustomed to seeing students lose score points after
   about fifteen minutes because they cannot concentrate their attenton any longer.

4. It is best to work first through all the questions
   or problems that one knows the answers to without
   hesitation or doubt. This is insurance that one
   will have an opportunity to try the tasks that are
   easy. If a question or problem is going to take
   some thought, come back to it later. This is the
   single most important know-how skill in taking
   tests. The painfully methodical person who cannot
   bear to leave a question unanswered before going
   to the next one is handicapped on a standardized
   test, especially if it is a speed test. On the
   other hand, flipping from question to question
   without giving each one a good try is unwise.

5. Students should be warned to read all the answer
   choices given for every question, even on the firs
   pass and on the questions they know without hesita
   tion. Making an answer choice without reading all
   the options is folly. The wrong answers among the
   options given often are the answers obtained by
   persons, who have not read the question accurately
   or completely. So, as insurance against the error
   of hasty reading of the question, the student
   should never fail to read all the answer choices.

6. On the second pass, in coming back to the question
   skipped on the first time over, the best way is to
   go at each question and its answer options like
   Sherlock Holmes-looking for clues. Eliminating the
   answer options you are pretty certain are wrong and
   then studying the remaining ones may reveal some
   forgotten clue in your head or in the question.
   the student narrows the options down to two, he ha

12

increased his odds for choosing the right answer
from one in five to one in two. Usually, the
correct answers to a lot of questions will become
clear when this technique has been applied, and
there will then be no need for guessing. Information will have been used to eliminate the wrong
answers and deduce the correct one—a perfectly
respectable procedure in all academic circles. If
the student is still stumped after a reasonable
time, it may be best to pass the question again and
leave it for a third round. If time is short and
he has narrowed his choices down to two or three,
he should mark the one that on the whole seems most
likely.

7. Procedure as to guessing should depend on what the
directions have said about guessing. If the directions indicate or the examiner has said specifical-
ly that a scoring penalty will be assessed for
every wrong answer, it is unwise to guess at an
answer unless the choices have been reduced to two
or three. If the guess must be among more options
in answer to a question, the odds are likely to be
against the guesser. BUT, if the directions say
nothing about a penalty for wrong answers, or if
they say only to "avoid wild guessing," or if they
say that the score will be the total of the correct
answers, it is wise to put down an answer for each
question.

8. If a student finished all questions in the test
before time is called, he should go back and study
again the questions about which he had the most
doubt. Here is a point at which too many students
pass up an opportunity for gaining another score
point or two. They heave a sigh of relief after
completing the second pass; think, "That's the best
I can do"; and quit. Almost always there is at least
one question that can be answered, or answered
better, given a little more attention.

9. You cannot fudge extra points by leaving small
pencil marks around on the machine-scorable answer
sheet. There was a time when scoring machines did
accumulate a few extra points from pencil marks
concealed in printed matter on the answer sheet,
but that time is long past. And the machine cannot
be fooled if two answers are put down in the case
of a doubtful choice. Scoring machines these days
read every pencil mark on the sheet, however,
faint, and consider its meaning; this may also

13

result in lost points. If there are two answer
marks for any question, real or accidental, the
machine will either ignore both of them, recognize
the darker mark, or subtract points for the double
marked question, depending on the particular
machine. Any such efforts to fool the machine will
not work and will also waste valuable time.

When tests are taken as they are intended to be taken,
as interesting job samples on which the student can try
out his hard-won skills, the process is stimulating for
most students and enjoyable for many. Learning is a
satisfying experience; and as testing is the proving part
of that experience, it, too, can be satisfying and enjoyable. More important than the satisfactions it gives
directly to student, though, is the guidance that good
testing gives to the teacher, the counselor, the admission
officer, and the student himself. (11: 178-184)

ANXIETY

STRESS

TENSION

RELAXATION

ANXIETY

STRESS | | TENSION

RELAXATION

Man is faced daily with stressors ranging from cuts,
bruises, and viruses to fatigue, fears and anxieties.
The body not only reacts to these in highly specific ways
but it also has a general response consisting of an
"alarm reaction" followed by a "stage of resistance" and
a "stage of exhaustion".

Situations which cause a strong emotional response can
lead to hyperactivity and neuromuscular tension in the
body. Repeated exposure to emotional stressors without
adequate adaption to these stressors may lead to mental
and physical illness. However, a situation which might be
stressful to one person is not necessarily stressful to
another. A multitude of hereditary and environmental
factors affect an individual's ability to adapt to specific stressors. Research evidence suggests that healthy
and physically fit persons can more easily adapt to
stressful situations.

Some muscular tension is necessary to keep us awake
and alert and ready to respond. A certain degree of
neuromuscular tension aids some types of mental activity
on the other hand, intellectual and emotional states are
usually accompained by an increase in muscular tension.
There seems to be an optimum level of tension to facilitate the thought process and its effect seems to vary
with individuals.

While smoking marijuana or drinking alcoholic bever-
ages tends to make one feel high and give off temporary
relief, there is no proven fact that it will cause one to
score high on a test. Therefore, excessive tension can
be avoided or relieved by proper planning of our daily
lives. Overly studying for an examination is as fatiguing
as fatigue from lack of rest and sleep, emotional strain
pain, or a disease. Moderation in all things may still
be a helpful adage. (5: 91-93)

ANXIETY AVOIDANCE

1. Develop a good attitude toward the test. To do well on an exam, you must think positively. Put everything else out of your mind and concentrate on the test item you are answering.

2. Be on time. Get up early enough so that you will not need to rush.

3. Go into the test situation alert but calm.

4. Pay careful attention to directions, determining clearly the nature of the task and the intended basis for response.

5. If you are unsure of what to do on the sample questions, ask for clarification.

6. Do not be concerned if you do not finish all the questions on the examinations.

Before a big important test, some tension relieving exercises are necessary for most people, although a relaxing exercise for one individual may be a boring exercise for another. On the following page are some exercises you may want to try to see if they might aid you in relaxing before a test, therefore having a positive effect on your being able to do your best. However, nothing beats knowing one's stuff.

..... (Screaming) scream to the top of your voice for
as long as you can. As a result you should feel
light-headed thereby causing you to think about
your light-headedness. Before you realize it so
of your tensions have subsided.

..... (Finger-Matching) place your ten fingers against
one another and placing your hands over your che
as you apply pressure inhale and count to twen
(20) then release your applied finger pressure a
exhale.

..... (Chair Lifts) take hold of both sides of your
chair inhale as you lift your body from the cha
(counting to fifteen), then turn loose and exha
causing your body to fall back onto the chair.

..... (Feet) place both feet together and apply press
to the floor with your toes as you hold your
breath to a (count of twenty-five) then, exhale
and quickly take a deep breath.

..... (Breathing) pant inhaling and exhaling for two
minutes.

..... (Eyes) close your eyes and pretend that you are
floating on a soft cloud and as you begin to fe
comfortable and relaxful, slowly open your eyes
trying to maintain the aforementioned feelings.

..... (Prayer) pray that fear and anxiety will no lon
plague you and that you will have complete control of your mind.

..... (Stand) stand up on both feet and stretch your
arms out over your head and <u>scream</u> as loud as
possible.

..... (Head) roll your head slowly in a large circle
first clockwise and then counter-clockwise.

..... (Shoulders) hunch the shoulders as high as
possible and then let them drop. Repeat seven
times.

..... (Always) the emphasis is placed on detecting th
feeling of tension as the first step in "lettin
go".

- Refresh yourself with a few, well-chosen rest pauses during the test.

- Use controlled association to see the relation of one question to another and with as many important ideas as you can develop.

TEST—TAKING MADE SIMPLE

- Now that you're a "cool" test-taker, stay calm and confident throughout the test. Don't let anything throw you.

- Edit, check, proofread your answers. Be a "Bitter-Ender." Stay working until they make you go.

BEFORE THE TEST

You're going to pass this examination because you ha
received the best possible preparation for it. But, un-
like many others, you're going to give the best possible
account of yourself by acquiring the rare skill of effec
tively using your knowledge to answer the examination
questions.

First off, get rid of any negative attitudes toward t
test. You have a negative attitude when you view the te
as a device to "trip you up" rather than an opportunity
show how effectively you have learned.

APPROACH THE TEST WITH SELF-CONFIDENCE

Plugging through this book was a mean job, and now th
you've done it you're probably better prepared than 90%
the others. Self-confidence is one of the biggest
strategic assets you can bring to the testing room.

Nobody likes tests, but some persons could permit
themselves to get upset or angry when they see what they
think is an unfair test. The expert doesn't. He keeps
calm and moves right ahead, knowing that everyone is tak
ing the same test. Anger, resentment, fear---they all
slow you down. "Grin and bear it!"

Besides, every test you take, including this one is a
valuable experience which improves your skill. Since y
will undoubtedly be taking other tests in the years to
come, it may help you to regard this one as training to
perfect your skill.

Keep calm; there's no point to panic. If you've done
your work there's no need for it; and if you haven't, a
cool head is your very first requirement.

Why be the frightened kind of student who enters the
examination chamber in a mental coma? A test taken unde
mental stress does not provide a fair measure of your
ability. At the very least, this book has removed for y
some of the fear and mystery that surrounds examinations
A certain amount of concern is normal and good, but
excessive worry saps your strength and keeness. In othe
words, be prepared EMOTIONALLY.

Pre-Test Review

If you know any others who are taking this test, you'll probably find it helpful to review the book and your notes with them. The group should be small, certainly not more than four. Team study at this stage should seek to review the material in a different way than you learned it originally; should strive for an exchange of ideas between you and the other members of the group; should be selective in sticking to important ideas; should stress the vague and unfamiliar rather than that which you all know well; should be business like and devoid of any nonsense; should end as soon as you get tired.

One of the <u>worst</u> strategies in test taking is to do all your preparation the night before the exam. As a reader of this book, you have scheduled and spaced your study properly so as not to suffer from the fatigue and emotional disturbance that comes from cramming the night before.

Cramming is a very good way to <u>guarantee poor test results</u>.

However, you would be wise to prepare yourself factually by <u>reviewing your notes</u> in the 48 hours preceding the exam. You shouldn't have to spend more than two or three hours in this way. Stick to salient points. The others will fall into place quickly.

Don't confuse cramming with a final, calm review which helps you focus on the significant areas of this book and further strengthens your confidence in your ability to handle the test questions. In other words, prepare yourself FACTUALLY.

Keep Fit

Mind and body work together. Poor physical condition will lower your mental efficiency in preparing for an examination, observe the common-sense rules of health. Get sufficient sleep and rest, eat proper foods, plan recreation and exercise. In relation to health and examinations, two cautions are in order. Don't miss your meals prior to an examination in order to get extra time for study, Likewise, don't miss your regular sleep by sitting up late to "cram" for the examination. Cramming is an attempt to learn in a very short period of time what should have been learned through regular and consistent study. Not only are these two habits detrimental to

health, but seldom do they pay off in terms of effective
learning. It is likely that you will be more confused
than better prepared on the day of the examination if yo
have broken into your daily routine by missing your meal
or sleep.

On the night before the examination go to bed at yo
regular time and try to get a good night's sleep. Don't
go to the movies. Don't date. In other words, prepare
yourself PHYSICALLY.

Several Hours Before

After a very light, leisurely meal get to the exami
nation room ahead of time, perhaps 30 minutes early . .
but not so early that you have time to get into an argument with others about what's going to be asked on the
exam, etc. The reason for coming early is to help you g
accustomed to the room. It will help you to a better
start.

Bring all necessary equipment . . .
. . .pen, two sharpened pencils, watch, paper, eraser,
ruler, and any other things you're instructed to bring.

Get settled . . .
. . . by finding your seat and staying in it. If no
special seats have been assigned, take one in the front
facilitate the seating of others coming after you.

The test will be given by a test supervisor who rea
the directions and otherwise tells you what to do. The
people who walk about passing out the test papers and
assisting the examination are test proctors. If you're
not able to see or hear properly notify the supervisor o
a proctor. If you have any other difficulites during th
examination, like a defective test booklet, scoring penc
answer sheet; or if it's too hot or cold or dark or draf
let them know. You're entitled to favorable test conditions.

Relax . . .
. . . and don't bring on unnecessary tenseness by worry
about the difficulty of the examination. If necessary w
a minute before beginning to write. If you are still
tense, take a couple of deep breaths, look over your tes
equipment, or do something which will take your mind aw
from the examination for a moment.

If your collar or shoes are tight, loosen them.

Put away unnecessary materials so that you have a good, clear space on your desk to write freely.

WHEN THE TEST ADMINISTRATOR SAYS "GO" - TAKE YOUR TIME!

Listen very carefully to the test supervisor. If you fail to hear something important that he says, you may not be able to read it in the written directions and may suffer accordingly.

If you don't understand the directions you have heard or read, raise your hand and inform the proctor. Read carefully the directions for each part of the test before beginning to work on that part. If you skip over such directions too hastily, you may miss a main idea and thus lose credit for an entire section.

Get an Overview of the Examination

After reading the directions carefully, look over the entire examination to get an over-view of the nature and scope of the test. The purpose of this over-view is to give you some idea of the nature, scope, and difficulty of the examination.

It has another advantage. An item might be so phrased that it sets in motion a chain of thought that might be helpful in answering other items on the examination.

Still another benefit to be derived from reading all the items before you answer any is that the few minutes involved in reading the items gives you an opportunity to relax before beginning the examination. This will make for better concentration. As you read over these items the first time, check those whose answers immediately come to you. These will be the ones you will answer first. Read each item carefully before answering. It is a good practice to read each item at least twice to be sure that you understand it.

Plan Ahead

In other words, you should know precisely where you
are going before you start. You should know:

1. Whether you have to answer all the questions or
   whether you can choose those that are easiest t
   you;

2. Whether all the questions are easy; (there may
   a pattern of difficult, easy, etc.)

3. The length of the test; the number of questions

4. The kind of scoring method used;

5. Which questions, if any, carry extra weight;

6. What types of questions are on the test;

7. What directions apply to each part of the test

8. Whether you must answer the questions consecu-
   tively.

Budget Your Time Strategically!

Quickly figure out how much of the allotted time y
can give to each section and still finish ahead of time
Don't forget to figure on the time you're investing in
overview. Then alter your schedule so that you can spe
more time on those parts that count most. Then, if you
can, plan to spend less time on the easier questions, s
that you can devote the time saved to the harder questions. Figuring roughly, you should finish half the
questions when half the allotted time has gone by. If
there are 100 questions and you have three hours, you
should have finished 50 questions after one and one hal
hours. So bring along a watch whether the instructions
call for one or not. Jot down your "exam budget" and
stick to it INTELLIGENTLY.

EXAMINATION STRATEGY

Probably the most important single stragety you ca
learn is to do the easy questions first. The very hard
questions should be read and temporarily postponed.
Identify them with a dot and return to them later.

This strategy has several advantages for you:

1. You are sure to get credit for all the questions you are sure of. If time runs out, you will have all the sure shots, losing out only on those which you might have missed anyway.

2. By reading and laying away the tough ones you give your subconscious a chance to work on them. You may be pleasantly surprised to find the answers to the puzzlers popping up for you as you deal with related questions.

3. You will not risk getting caught by the time limit just as you reach a question you know really well.

A Tested Tactic

It is inadvisable on some examinations to answer each question in the order presented. The reason for this is that some examiners design tests so as to extract as much mental energy from you as possible. They put the most difficult questions at the beginning, the easier questions last. Or they may vary difficult with easy questions in a fairly regular pattern right through the test. Your survey of the test should reveal the pattern and your strategy for dealing with it.

If difficult questions appear at the beginning, answer them until you feel yourself slowing down or getting tired. Then switch to an easier part of the examination. You will return to the difficult portion after you have rebuilt your confidence by answering a batch of easy questions. Knowing that you have a certain number of points "under your belt" will help you when you return to the more difficult questions. You will answer them with a much clearer mind; and you will be refreshed by the change of pace.

Time

Use your time wisely. It is an important element in your test and you must use every minute effectively, working as rapidly as you can without sacrificing accuracy. Your exam survey and budget will guide you in dispensing your time. Wherever you can, pick up seconds on the easy ones. Devote it to those which give you the most points.

Relax Occasionally and Avoid Fatigue

If the exam is long (two or more hours) give yourse short rest periods as you feel you need them. If you ar not permitted to leave the room, relax in your seat, loo up from your paper, rest your eyes, stretch your legs, shift your body. Take several deep breaths and get back job, refreshed. If you do not do this you run the risk getting nervous and tightening up. Your thinking may be hampered and you may make a few unnecessary mistakes.

Do not become worried or discouraged if the examina tion seems difficult to you. The questions in the vario fields are purposely made difficult and searching so tha the examination will discriminate effectively even among superior students. No one is expected to get a perfect or near-perfect score.

Remember that if the examination seems difficult to you, it may be even more difficult for your neighbor.

Think!

This is not a joke because you are not an IBM machi Nobody is able to write all the time and also to read an think through each question. You must plan each answer. Do not give hurried answers in an atmosphere of panic. Even though you see a lot of questions, remember that th are objective and not very time-consuming. Do not rush headlong through questions that must be thought through.

Edit, Check, Proofread . . .

. . .after completing all the questions. Invariably, yo will find some foolish errors which you need not have ma and which you can easily correct. Do not just sit back or leave the room ahead of time. Read over your answers and make sure you wrote exactly what you meant to write. And that you wrote the answers in the right place. You might even find that you have omitted some answers inad tently. You have budgeted time for this job of proofre ing. PROOFREAD and pick up points.

One word of caution. Do not count on making major changes. And do not go in for wholesale changing of answers. To arrive at your answers in the first place y have read carefully and thought correctly. Second-guess ing at this stage is more likely to result in wrong an- swers. So do not make changes unless you are quite cert you were wrong in the first place.

FOLLOW DIRECTIONS CAREFULLY

In answering questions on the objective or short-form examination, it is most important to follow all instructions carefully. Unless you have marked the answers properly, you will not receive credit for them. In addition, even in the same examination, the instructions will not be consistent. In one section you may be urged to guess if you are not certain; in another you may be cautioned against guessing. Some questions will call for the best choice among four or five alternatives; others may ask you to select the one incorrect or the least probable answer.

On some tests you will be provided with worked out fore-exercises, complete with correct answers. However, avoid the temptation to skip the directions and begin working just from reading the model questions and answers. Even though you may be familiar with the particular type of questions, the directions may be different from those which you had followed previously. If the type of question should be new to you, work through the model until you understand it perfectly. This may save you time, and earn you a higher rating on the examination.

If the directions for the examination are written, read them carefully, at least twice. If the directions are given orally, listen attentively and then follow them precisely. For example, if you are directed to use plus (+) and minus (-) to mark true-false items, then do not use "T" and "F". If you are instructed to "blacken" a space on machine-scored tests, do not use a check (✓) or an "X". Make all symbols legible, and be sure that they have been placed in the proper answer space. It is easy, for example, to place the answer for item 5 in the space reserved for item 6. If this is done, then all of your following answers may be wrong. It is also very important that you understand the method they will use in scoring the examination. Sometimes they tell you in the directions. The method of scoring may affect the amount of time you spend on an item, especially if some items count more than others. Likewise, the directions may indicate whether or not you should guess in case you are not sure of the answer. Some methods of scoring penalize you for guessing.

Cue Words. Pay special attention to qualifying word or phrases in the directions. Such words as <u>one, best</u> reason, surest, means most nearly the same as, preferable least correct, etc., all indicate that <u>one</u> response is called for, and that you must select the response which best fits the qualifications in the question.

Time. Sometimes a time limit is set for each section of the examination. If that is the case, follow the time instructions carefully. Your <u>exam budget</u> and your watch can help you here. Even if you have not finished a section when the time limit is up, pass on to the next section. The examination has been planned according to the time schedule.

If the examination paper bears the instruction "Do not turn over page until signal is given," or "Do not start until signal is given," follow the instruction. Otherwise, you may be disqualified.

Pay Close Attention. Be sure you understand what you are doing at all times. Especially in dealing with true-false or multiple-choice questions it is vital that you understand the meaning of every question. It is normal to be working under stress when taking an examination, and it is easy to skip a word or jump to a false conclusion, which may cost you points on the examination. In many multiple-choice and matching questions, the examiners deliberately insert plausible-appearing false answers in order to catch the candidate who is not alert.

Answer clearly. If the examiner who marks your paper cannot understand what you mean, you will not receive credit for your correct answer. On a True-False examination you will not receive any credit for a question which is marked both true and false. If you are asked to underline be certain that your lines are under and not through the words and that they do not extend beyond them. When using the separate answer sheet it is important <u>when you decide to change an answer</u>, you erase the first answer completely. If you leave any graphite from the pencil on the wrong space it will cause the scoring machine to cancel the right answer for that question.

Watch your "Weights." If the examination is "weighted" it means that some parts of the examination are considered more important than others and rated more highly. For instance, you may find that the instructions will indicate "Part I, Weight 50; Part II, Weight 25, Part III Weight 25." In such a case, you would devote half of your time to the first part, and divide the second half of your time among Parts II and III.

A Funny Thing . . .
. . . happened to you on your way to the bottom of the totem pole. You <u>thought</u> the right answer but you marked the <u>wrong</u> one.

1. You <u>mixed answer symbols</u>! You decided (rightly) that Baltimore (Choice D) was correct. Then you marked B (for Baltimore) instead of D.

2. You <u>misread</u> a simple instruction! Asked to give the <u>latest</u> word in a scrambled sentence, you correctly arranged the sentence, and then marked the letter corresponding to the <u>earliest</u> word in that miserable sentence.

3. You <u>inverted digits</u>! Instead of the correct number, 96, you wrote (or read) 69.

Funny, Tragic! Stay away from accidents.

Record your answers on the answer sheet one by one as you answer the questions. Care should be taken that these answers are recorded next to the appropriate numbers on your answer sheet. It is poor practice to write your answers first on the test booklet and then to transfer them all at one time to the answer sheet. This procedure causes many errors. And then, how would you feel if you ran out to time before you had a chance to transfer all the answers.

When and How to Guess

Read the directions carefully to determine the scoring method that will be used. In some tests, the directions will indicate that guessing is advisable if you do not know the answer to a question. In such tests, only the right answers are counted in determining your score. If such is the case, do not omit any items. If you do not know the answer, or if you are not sure of your answer, then <u>guess</u>.

On the other hand, if the directions state that a scoring formula <u>will</u> be used in determining your score or that you are <u>not to guess</u>, then <u>omit</u> the question if you do not know <u>the answer</u>, or if you are not sure of the answer. When the scoring formula is used, a percentage of the <u>wrong</u> answers will be subtracted from the number of right answers as a correction for haphazard guessing. It is improbable, therefore, that mere guessing will improve your score significantly. It may even lower your score. Another disadvantage in guessing under such circumstances is that it consumes valuable time that you might profitably use in answering the questions you know.

If, however, you are uncertain of the correct answer but have some knowledge of the question and are able to eliminate one or more of the answer choices as wrong, you chance of getting the right answer is improved, and it will be to your advantage to answer such a question rather than omit it.

BEAT THE ANSWER SHEET

Even though you have had plenty of practice with the answer sheet used on machine-scored examinations, we must give you a few more, last-minute pointers.

The present popularity of tests requires the use of electrical test scoring machines. With these machines, scoring which would require the labor of several men for hours can be handled by one man in a fraction of the time.

The scoring machine is an amazingly intricate and helpful device, but the machine is not human. The machine cannot, for example, tell the difference between an intended answer and a stray pencil mark, and will count both indiscriminately. The machine cannot count a pencil mark if the pencil mark is not brought in contact with the electrodes. For these reasons, specially printed answer sheets with response spaces properly located and properly filled in must be employed. Since not all pencil leads contain the necessary ingredients, a special pencil must be used and a heavy solid mark must be made to indicate answers.

(a) Each pencil mark must be heavy and black. Light marks should be traced with the special pencil

(b) Each mark must be in the space between the pair of dotted lines and entirely fill this space.

(c) All stray pencil marks on the paper, clearly not intended as answers, must be completely erased

(d) Each question must have only one answer indicated. If multiple answers occur, all extraneous marks should be thoroughly erased. Otherwise, the machine will give you no credit for your correct

30

answer.
Be sure to use the special electrographic pencil!

Your answer sheet is the only one that reaches the
office where papers are scored. For this reason it is
important that the blanks at the top be filled in completely and correctly. The proctors will check this, but just
in case they slip up, make certain yourself that your
paper is complete.

Many exams caution competitors against making any
marks on the test booklet itself. Obey that caution even
though it goes against your grain to work neatly. If you
work neatly and obediently with the test booklet you will
probably do the same with the answer sheet. And that pays
off in high scores. (9: 408-413)

HERE'S HOW TO MARK YOUR ANSWERS
ON
MACHINE-SCORED ANSWER SHEETS:

EXAMPLES

MAKE ONLY ONE MARK FOR EACH ANSWER. ADDITIONAL AND
STRAY MARKS MAY BE COUNTED AS MISTAKES.   IN MAKING
CORRECTIONS, ERASE ERRORS COMPLETELY. MAKE GLOSSY BLACK
MARKS.

RATIONALE FOR TESTS GIVEN

College Placement Test scores are used to place students at the appropriate level of study in college. Freshmen entering college differ considerably with respect to achievement in various subject areas. Some students will profit from advanced training in a particular subject, some will require remedial work, and others will be best prepared for the conventional beginning course. A placement program should be directed toward identifying the appropriate level of study for each entering freshman.

The most practical approach for determining this level is to compare the achievement of each student with that of other students in the course for which he is eligible. If his knowledge of a particular subject is considerably less than that of the majority beginning the freshman course, he should be assigned to a remedial class. If his grasp of the subject is as thorough as that of the better students who are entering an advanced course, he might skip the beginning course. If his achievement falls between these two levels, he should be assigned to the first-year-course-if possible, with students whose level of attainment is similar to his.

The principal advantage of a testing program conducted by the college is that, since all students take the same test, they can be compared against a common standard. When secondary school averages are compared, it is necessary to consider the differences among schools and their grading practices. Further, secondary school records do not ordinarily indicate the emphasis given to particular topics within a subject area; inspection of a placement test insures the selection of a testing instrument pertinent to specific topics.

To gain information and pleasure, reading is basic to every subject area. The Iowa Silent Reading Test is designed to measure whether the student is able to comprehend rapidly and indicate by specific reactions his understanding of the material. The test is a reliable, accurate source for measuring the desired abilities and identifying important weaknesses in order to make effective improvement in reading.

According to the grade placements made by new students as they enter the college, the student is placed in an area which the test indicates will be to his benefit. At the end of the semester, students in Reading classes are re-tested and placed accordingly.

33

The English Composition Test is designed to measure student's ability to recognize and apply principles of good writing. It strives to test sensitivity in reading and skill in manipulating language, on the assumption that these activities are closely related to good writing. If students meet the necessary requirement they are placed in the basic college English program.

The School and College Ability Test (SCAT) aid in estimating the capacity of a student to undertake the academic work of the particular level of schooling. They measure the two kinds of school-related abilities which are most important in the greatest number of school and college endeavors: verbal and quantitative. If students score well in the quantitative section of the SCAT they are able to meet the Math requirements for their curriculum. If not, they are required to register for basic Math.

The Survey of Study Habits and Attitudes was developed to measure study methods, motivation for studying and certain attitudes toward scholastic activities. Its purposes are: (1) to identify students whose study habits and attitudes are different from those of students who earn high grades, (2) to aid in understanding students with academic difficulties, and (3) to provide a basis for helping such students improve their study habits and attitudes and thus more fully realize their best potential. The results are reported to departments and answer sheets given to Counseling Services for conferences with students.

The California Language Test, used for English 052 Objective Final Examination, shows the extent of student mastery of the fundamental skills in terms of various derived scores. It measures the ability of the student to make intelligent use of the facts and skills at his disposal to solve new problems, to make inferences, and to draw conclusions. After, taking the test as a part of their final examination, students are placed accordingly.

The primary use of The New Purdue Placement Tests in English is to assess the knowledge possessed by students what is called "good English." They are used at the college as a means for placing students in courses of study appropriate to their strenghts and deficiencies.

Reading and written expression are two of the fundamental areas measured by The 1960 Cooperative English Test used for English 102 Final Examination.

The Scholastic Aptitude Test (SAT) measures developed verbal and mathematical reasoning abilities that are important for academic performance in college. The verbal questions measure your ability to understand what you read and the extent of your vocabulary. The mathematical questions measure quantitative abilities closely related to college work. The SAT is a necessary requirement for admission to the college.

The Graduate Record Examinations are designed to give the graduate schools information concerning your educational background and general scholastic ability. The GRE Aptitude Test measures general verbal, quantitative, and analytical abilities that are important for academic achievement.

The National Teacher Examinations (NTE) are standardized, secure tests that provide objective measures of academic achievement for college seniors completing teacher education programs and for advanced candidates who have received additional training in specific fields.

Mathematics Skills Test is a test of basic arithmetic concepts and computations designed to determine one's strengths and weaknesses in the important skill areas of fractions, decimals, and per cents. The results of this test will provide useful information for (1) placing one in the proper mathematics course and (2) planning one's college level remediation program if needed.

SAMPLE TEST QUESTIONS

Cooperative School

and

College Ability Tests

GENERAL DIRECTIONS

This is a test of some of the skills you have been learning ever since you first entered school. You should take it in the same way that you would work on any other new and interesting assignment.

The test is divided into four parts, which you will take one at a time. Give each one your close attention and do your best on every question. You probably will find some of the questions quite easy and others more difficult. You are not expected to answer every question correctly.

There are a few general rules for taking this test that will help you to earn your best score:

- Work carefully, but do not spend too much time on any one question. It usually is better to answer first all of the questions in the part that you know well and can answer quickly. Then go back to the questions that you want to think about.

- If you work at average speed you will have plenty of time to read and answer all of the questions. By leaving until last the questions that are most difficult, you will make best use of your time.

- You may answer questions even when you are not perfectly sure that your answers are correct. Your score will be the number of correct answers you mark.

- Put all of your answers on the answer sheet. This test booklet should not be marked in any way. Your examiner will give you an extra sheet of scratch paper to use when you do the number problems.

- Fill in all the information called for on the answer sheet and PRINT your name so that it can be read.

- Make sure that you understand instructions before you start work on any part. Ask the examiner to repeat the instructions if you do not understand exactly what you are to do.

- Make your answer marks on the answer sheet heavy and black. If you change your mind about an answer, be sure to erase your first mark completely.

If you give this test your best effort, your score will provide a good estimate of your ability in these important skills.

DIRECTIONS FOR PART I

Each question in Part I consists of a sentence in which
word is missing; a blank indicates where the word has be
removed from the sentence. Beneath each sentence are fi
words, one of which is the missing word. You are to sel
the missing word by deciding which one of the five words
best fits in with the meaning of the sentence.

1. Since the neighboring towns could not consume the en
   tire production of the farms, the chief problem of t
   farmers was to find adequate ( ).

   A. crops B. income C. credit D. laborers
   E. markets

2. Many citizens of Washington, D.C., wanted the right
   vote so that they could be ( ) in national affairs.

   F. well-known G. reasonable H. influenced
   J. represented K. undivided

3. The man who is born poor generally stays poor unless
   has extraordinary ( ).

   A. interest B. talent C. honesty D. sincerity
   E. instinct

4. He dealt ( ) with them because their conduct appealed
   his heart.

   F. justly G. competently H. quickly J. lenier
   K. vigorously

5. His knowledge of human frailty prevents him from bei
   too ( ) about the future of modern society.

   A. optimistic B. angry C. informative
   D. dogmatic E. discouraging

38

DIRECTIONS FOR PART II

There are five problems in Part II of the test. Following each problem there are five suggested answers. Work each problem in your head or on a piece of scratch paper. Then look at the five suggested answers and decide which one is correct. Blacken the space under its letter on the answer sheet.

1. .09 X .09

   A. .0081
   B. .081
   C. .81
   D. 1
   E. None of these

2. $\frac{8}{15} \div \frac{2}{3}$

   F. $\frac{16}{45}$

   G. $\frac{11}{17}$

   H. $\frac{4}{5}$

   J. $\frac{5}{4}$

   K. $\frac{45}{16}$

3. 50,007
   −2,698

   A. 47,309
   B. 48,409
   C. 48,419
   D. 57,309
   E. None of these

4. 3 $\frac{5}{6}$
    6 $\frac{2}{3}$
   +5 $\frac{1}{6}$

   F. 14 $\frac{2}{3}$

   G. 15 $\frac{1}{2}$

   H. 15 $\frac{2}{3}$

   J. 15 $\frac{5}{6}$

   K. None of these

5. 3 $\frac{1}{2}$ ÷ 3 $\frac{1}{2}$

   A. 0
   B. 1
   C. $\frac{4}{49}$
   D. $\frac{49}{4}$
   E. None of these

39

DIRECTIONS FOR PART III

Each of the questions in Part III consists of one word in large letters followed by five words or phrases in small letters. Read the word in large letters. Then pick, from the words or phrases following it, the one whose meaning closest to the word in large letters.

1. LOITER

   A. split
   B. linger
   C. soil
   D. lighten
   E. restrain

2. APPAREL

   F. clothing
   G. equipment
   H. vision
   J. attitude
   K. curtain

3. RAMBLE

   A. stagger
   B. speak indistinctly
   C. entangle
   D. wander about
   E. mix up

4. BLEMISH

   F. redden
   G. snub
   H. mar
   J. defame
   K. squander

5. BALK

   A. come to one's senses
   B. bring under control
   C. follow after
   D. stop up an opening
   E. refuse to move

SAMPLE TEST QUESTIONS

College Placement Test

DIRECTIONS

For each question, choose the best answer and blacken the corresponding space on the answer sheet.
Each question below consists of a word in capital letters followed by five lettered words or phrases. Choose the word or phrase that is most nearly <u>opposite</u> in meaning to the word in capital letters. Since some of the questions require you to distinguish fine shades of meaning, consider all the choices before deciding which is best.

1. BABBLE: (a) irrigation (b) pollution
   (c) meaningful speech (d) useful object
       (e) helpful person

2. UNWARRANTED: (a) repaired (b) elaborate
   (c) satisfied (d) languid (e) justified

3. PROLIFIC: (a) unproductive (b) unhealthy
   (c) retarded (d) diminutive (e) eratic

4. EFFUSIVENESS: (a) reticence (b) refinement
   (c) narrow-mindedness (d) lack of success
   (e) inability to adjust

DIRECTIONS

Each sentence below has one or two blanks, each blank
indicating that something has been omitted. Beneath the
sentence are five lettered words or sets of words. Choose
the word or set of words that best fits the meaning of the
sentence as a whole.

1. The distemper virus does not infect humans, and many
    of the usual experimental animals such as rabbits,
    guinea pigs, and white rats are also --- to infection

    (a) susceptible (b) resistant (c) opposed
    (d) hostile   (e) responsive

2. Hume's portrait of Cromwell is irremediably-----:
    he says on page one what he ------ in later pages.

    (a) suggestive..reveals
    (b) impressionistic..imagines
    (c) abbreviated..refutes
    (d) tedious..omits
    (e) inconsistent..denies

3. Despite a ----- of long-range remedies and stopgap
    efforts, the problem of poverty continues to grow
    more desperate.

    (a) famine (b) paucity (c) reversal (d) cessation
    (e) plethora

43

DIRECTIONS

Each question below consists of a related pairs of words or phrases, followed by five lettered paris of words or phrases. Select the lettered pair that <u>best</u> expresses a relationship similar to that expressed in the original pair.

1. CHOIR:SINGERS:

   (a)   victory:soldiers
   (b)   class:teachers
   (c)   crowd:protesters
   (d)   challenge:duelists
   (e)   orchestra:musicians

2. DRUNKARD:INEBRIATED::

   (a)   dolt:wise
   (b)   brute:stunned
   (c)   faddist:outmoded
   (d)   optimist:hopeful
   (e)   busybody:confused

3. CULL:SELECTIVE::

   (a)   muffle:abrasive
   (b)   winnow:negative
   (c)   refine:primitive
   (d)   separate:relative
   (e)   demolish:destructive

DIRECTIONS

The passage below is followed by questions based on its content. Answer all questions following the passage on the basis of what is <u>stated</u> or <u>implied</u> in the passage.

(The passage for this test has been adapted from published material. The ideas contained in the passage are those of the original author and do not necessarily represent the opinions of the College Board of Educational Testing Service.)

The behavioral sciences are making rapid strides in the understanding, prediction, and control or behavior. In important ways we know how to select individuals who will exhibit certain behaviors and to establish conditions in groups which will lead to various predictable group behaviors; in animals our ability to understand, predict, and control goes even further, possibly foreshadowing future steps in relation to man.

There is every reason to believe that the same sequence of events will occur in the behavioral sciences. First, the public ignores or views with disbelief; then, as it discovers that the findings of a science are more dependable than theories based on common sense, it begins to use them; eventually, the widespread use of these findings creates a tremendous demand. Finally, the development of the science spirals upward at an ever-increasing rate. Consequently, even though the findings of the behavioral sciences are not widely used today, there is every likelihood that they will be widely used tomorrow.

1.   The author suggests that the next change in the public's attitude toward behavioral science will lead the public to

(a) ignore the findings
(b) increase the use of the findings
(c) disbelieve the findings
(d) use these findings against each other
(e) lose interest in the findings

2.   The tone of this passage can best be described as

(a)   condescending   (c)   insipid
(b)   humble   (d)   admonitory
                  (d)   inspiring

45

SAMPLE QUESTIONS

Iowa Silent Reading Test

DIRECTIONS. This is a test to see how well and how rapidly
you can read silently. Read the story below very carefully
so that you can answer questions about it.

    At the end of <u>one minute</u> you will hear the word "Stop."
Put a circle around the word you are then reading and wait
for further instructions.

[1]Rubber is a substance composed of carbon and hydrogen
obtained from a milky liquid known as latex. [2]Latex comes
from the roots, stems, branches, leaves, and fruit of a
wide variety of trees. [3]For the most part these trees grow
in the tropics. [4]The milky juice is not the true sap, but
a secretion which does not seem to be essential to the life
of the plant. [5]If this liquid is allowed to stand for a
few hours, the particles of rubber rise to the surface.
[6]The doughy mass thus obtained can easily be rolled into a
sheet or other convenient form. [7]When allowed to dry, it
loses its doughy character and becomes the firm, elastic
solid known as raw or crude rubber.

[8]In whatever form the crude rubber comes to the factory,
the first thing that must be done is to clean it thoroughly
and test it, as rubber varies greatly in composition.
[9]Until it is used it is stored in a cool, dark place,
usually underground. [10]When a load is brought to the manu-
facturing plant, the first step is to steam it into a soft,
plastic mass.

DIRECTIONS. Without looking at the story you have just
read, answer these questions about it. You will have <u>two
minutes</u> for this work.

    Read each question and the answers given below it.
Select the correct answer. Notice the number of this
correct answer. In the spaces at the right fill the space
under this number

1. What is meant by the vulcanization process?
    1. adding chemicals   2. purifying the rubber
                   3. curing by heat

2. What is the name of the liquid from which rubber is
    made?
    1. sap   2. latex   3. secretion

3. How are the particles of rubber separated from the
    liquid?
    1. by allowing it to stand 2. by stirring it
                   3. by heating it

DIRECTIONS. A story is given below, with each sentence numbered. These numbers are to help you answer questions about the story. Read each question and find the sentence in the story which answers it. Notice the number of this sentence. Find this number among the answer spaces at the right of the questions and fill in the space under it.

GLASS

[1]Glass is made by melting sand with lime, potash, soda, or oxide of lead at a great heat. [2]Silica, which is the basis of sand, enters into all varieties of glass. [3]It has more to do with determining the quality than any of the other ingredients. [4]The purity of the ingredients and the proportion in which they are mixed also have much to do with the quality of the glass.

[5]Sand may be said to form the basis of the glass. [6]Consequently the clearness of the glass depends largely upon the quality of this ingredient. [7]The proportion of silica varies in different kinds of glass. [8]In lead glass it is from 42 to 60 per cent; olate contains about 79 per cent; and window glass about 70 per cent. [9]The amount of silica usually determines the degree of hardness, though other substances have some effect upon this quality. [10]Lead tends to make glass soft. Sometimes lime is used make it hard.[11]

1. What one substance is always present in some form in all kinds of glass?

2. What two factors in the manufacture of glass greatly affect its quality?

3. What effect does the quality of sand have on glass?

4. Is silica used in the same amounts in different varieties of glass?

5. What substance used in glass making tends to make the glass less brittle?

DIRECTIONS. This is a test of your ability to read and
interpret poetry. Read the poem below very carefulfy
before attempting to answer any of the questions about it.

Notice that in this selection certain passages are marked by numbered brackets. Read each question and find the
bracketed passage which contains the best answer to the
question. Answer the question by filling in the answer
space at the end of the question which has the same number
as the bracketed passage which contains the correct answer.

You may re-read parts of the poem if necessary.

AUTUMN

Season of mists and mellow fruitfulness,[1]
Close bosom-friend of the maturing sun; [2]
Conspiring with him how to load and bless[3]
With fruit the vines that 'round the thatch-eaves run;[4]
To bend with apples the moss'd cottage-trees,[5]
And fill all fruit with ripeness to the core;[6]
To swell the gourd, and plum the hazed shells[7]
With a sweet kernel; to set budding more[8]
And still more, later flowers for the bees,[9]
Until they think warm days will never cease;[10]
For summer has o'erbrimm'd their clammy cells.[11]
Who hath not seen Thee oft mid thy store?[12]

1. What are the sun and the season planning to do to the
   grapevines?

2. What are the attributes of this season of the year?

3. How does the autumn show that the harvest time is near?

4. How does the poet tell you that the apple trees are old
   and large?

5. For what purpose do the late flowers grow?

6. Does the poet think that everyone has seen the season
   of which he writes?

From "To Autumn," by John Keats

DIRECTIONS. The following exercise consists of a statement which is correctly completed by one of the five numbered words or phrases. Find the number of this correct
answer. Then, in the answer space at the right of the
exercise, fill in the space which has the same number as
the word or phrase you selected.

1. Tariff means—
   1. figure 2. personal expense 3. tax 4. ransom
   5. quotation

2. Naturalization means—
   1. nationalism 2. nationalization 3. international
   4. receiving the rights and privileges of a citizen
   5. receiving immigrants

3. To inaugurate means to—
   1. imprison 2. induct into office 3. fine
   4. exempt 5. incite to riot

4. Science means—
   1. systematized knowledge 2. theory 3. scientific
   4. general law 5. a scientist

5. Saturated means—
   1. completely filled 2. satisfied 3. dried
   4. expanded 5. developed

DIRECTIONS. You are to read each sentence and answer it
by filling in the answer space under the right answer.

1. Should the laws operate with equal effect on all
   people?

2. Is harmony between nations encouraged by the League of
   Nations?

3. Is dependable evidence always available?

4. Is it wise to misapply talent?

5. Do nations always react favorably to plans for reduc-
   tion of arms?

6. Does success usually depend on one's perseverance?

DIRECTIONS. Read each paragraph carefully, and then
study the questions A, B, and C. Select the correct
answer.

Before the match was invented, starting a fire was not
an easy matter. The Indians often started fires by rubb-
ing two sticks together. A much more common method among
the early settlers was to strike steel and flint together,
the sparks lighting a bit of "tinder." Often times live
coals were carried from one house to another. Since the
invention of the friction match in 1827, starting a fire
has become a simple process.

A. Choose the best title for the paragraph.
    1. Invention of Matches 2. Methods of Starting Fires
                    3. How Indians Started Fires

B. In case a pioneer was forced to build a fire while in
    camp, what did he use to start it?
    1. flint and steel 2. matches 3. coals from
                                          another fire

C. Indians often started fires by-
    1. striking two rocks together 2. rubbing two
                                          sticks together
                3. carrying burning tinder with them

DIRECTIONS. The answers to the questions are found in the
index below. First read the question and then find the
desired answer by looking under the proper topic in the
index. Then locate your answer among the possible answers given.

INDEX

51

QUESTIONS

1. On what page can you find a map of Africa?
   1. 90   2. 99   3. 119   4. 125   5. 130

2. Does the index tell where to find information about the
   value of cotton crop?   1. Yes   2. No

3. On what page can a definition of chemistry be found?
   1. 63   2. 66   3. 69   4. 70   5. 90

DIRECTIONS. This is a test of your ability to choose key
words for use in looking up information in an index. Read
each question and note that four numbered words or phrases
are given below it. Three of these words or phrases would
if looked up in an index, be likely to lead to an answer
to the question. One of the numbered parts would <u>not</u> help
in locating the information. Locate this one word or
phrase, <u>the one that would not help</u>, and note its number.

1. What is the value of our annual supply of mineral
   products?

   1. iron   2. lumber   3. mineral products   4. coal

2. What are the main water routes of the United States?

   1. canals   2. rivers   3. lakes   4. rainfall

3. Was John Hay a joint author of the treaty which defined
   the use of the Panama Canal?

   1. John Hay   2. secretary   3. Panama Canal
   4. Hay-Pauncefote Treaty

4. Was Pershing commander of the allied armies during the
   World War?

   1. general   2. Pershing   3. World War   4. Allies
                                                   armies

5. What is the annual cost of damage done to crops by
   insects?

   1. insects   2. boll weevil   3. wool   4. crops

SAMPLE QUESTIONS

English Composition

1. Alexander Hamilton and Thomas Jefferson ( ) divergent political theories.

   A. admitted to   C. concurred in
   B. assented to   D. subscribed to

2. The shelves of any drugstore are ( ) with creams, powders, lipsticks, skin tonics, wrinkle removers, and fingernail beautifiers.

   E. literally crawling   G. laden
   F. filled to the brim   H. amassed

3. An American pilot in Australia ( ).

   A. had one of the most unusual and dangerous air adventures ever reported

   B. had one of the most unusual and dangerous air adventures ever reported, and in which he was the central figure

   C. had one of the most unusual air adventures ever reported and, in addition, it was dangerous as well

   D. was the central figure where one of the most unusual and dangerous air adventures that has ever been reported happened

4. His intense desire to be sucessful in this one endeavor was so great that it ( ) a natural tendency to be lazy and indifferent.

   E. excelled   G. outdid
   F. outmaneuvered   H. overcame

5. The Song of Solomon is ( ) literally by many people.

   A. interpreted   C. translated
   B. expounded   D. defined

DIRECTIONS. Read each three-line sentence and decide
whether there are errors in usage, spelling, punctuation,
or capitalization in any of the three parts. If so, note
the letter printed beside the part which contains the
error or errors. Then mark the letter for that part next
to the number of the question on your answer sheet. If
there is no error in any part of the sentence, mark O on
your answer sheet. No sentence has more than one part
with errors, and some sentences do not have any errors.

1. A Unless the wire is fastened secure to the terminal,
   B there are reasons to believe that the connection
   C will eventually cause serious difficulty.

2. E It made no difference to Dr. Hampton whether Amy
   F chose the Christmas or Easter vacation period so
   G long as she had the operation within the next six
      months.

3. A One should not blame him greatly
   B on account of him being slow, but I
   C confess that I find his laziness unforgivable.

4. E Less members volunteered for the drive than
   F the director could have wished, but he knew
   G no tactful way to alleviate the situation.

5. A Across the room he glimpsed someone, who looked
   B just like his former employer; however, he
   C learned later that the man was a stranger.

SAMPLE QUESTIONS

The Survey of Study Habits and Attitudes

DIRECTIONS

The purpose of this survey is to furnish an inventory of study habits and attitudes to serve as a foundation for self-improvement. If taken seriously, this inventory can help you obtain a better understanding of how to study properly. If you will honestly and thoughtfully mark all of the statements on the pages that follow, you will be able to learn many of your study faults. The value of this survey to you will be in direct proportion to the care with which you mark each statement. Since your answers will be treated with the strictest confidence, feel free to answer all questions frankly.

You will mark your answers on a separate answer sheet. Make no marks on this booklet. For each statement a five-point scale is provided for indicating whether you rarely, sometimes, frequently, generally, or almost always do or feel as the statement suggests. You are to rate yourself on each statement by marking the space on your answer sheet that represents your answer choice. Thus, for example, you would mark space R on your answer sheet if you rarely follow the procedure described or if you feel that the statement is rarely true for you. In marking your answers, be sure that the number of the statement agrees with the number on the answer sheet. Make sure that your marks are heavy and black. Make no stray marks on the answer sheet and erase completely any mark that you wish to change.

To aid you in answering this questionnaire, the terms have been defined on a percentage basis as follows:

R - RARELY means from 0 to 15 per cent of the time.
S - SOMETIMES means from 16 to 35 per cent of the time.
F - FREQUENTLY means from 36 to 65 per cent of the time.
G - GENERALLY means from 66 to 85 per cent of the time.
A - ALMOST ALWAYS means from 86 to 100 per cent of the time.

Remember, you are asked to rate yourself, not in accordance with what you think you should do or feel, or as you think others might do or feel, but as you yourself are in the habit of doing and feeling. When you cannot answer a statement on the basis of actual experience, mark the statement according to what you would be likely to do if the situation should arise.

57

There are no "right" or "wrong" answers to these
statements, and there is no time limit for this questionnaire. Work as rapidly as you can without being careless
and do not spend too much time on any one statement.
Please do not omit any of the statements.

R—RARELY   S—SOMETIMES F—FREQUENTLY G—GENERALLY
            A—ALMOST ALWAYS

1. When my assigned homework is extra long or unusually
    difficult, I either quit in disgust or study only the
    easier parts of the lesson.

2. In preparing reports, themes, term papers, etc., I
    make certain that I clearly understand what is wanted
    before I begin work.

3. I feel that teachers lack understanding of the needs
    and interests of students.

4. My dislike for certain teachers causes me to neglect
    my school work.

5. When I get behind in my school work for some unavoid-
    able reason, I make up back assignments without
    prompting from the teacher.

6. Difficulty in expressing myself in writing slows me
    down on reports, themes, examinations, and other work
    to be turned in.

7. My teachers succeed in making their subjects interes
    ing and meaningful to me.

8. I feel that I would study harder if I were given mor
    freedom to choose courses that I like.

9. Daydreaming about dates, future plans, etc., distrac
    my attention from my lessons while I am studying.

10. My teachers criticize my written reports as being
    hastily written or poorly organized.

SAMPLE QUESTIONS

The California Language Test

INSTRUCTIONS TO STUDENTS:

This is a language test. In taking it you will show what
you know about capitalization, punctuation, and words and
sentences, and how well you can spell. No one is expected to do the whole test correctly, but you should answer
as many items as you can. Work as fast as you can without making mistakes.

******

DIRECTIONS: In most lines of the story and sentences
below, four words have a number above the first letter.
If ONE of the letters should be a capital, mark its
number. If none of the four letters should be a capital,
mark N, which stands for None. Not more than one letter
with a number over it should be a capital on any one line

1. One of the most interesting courses
       1   2   3   4

    1 2   3   4
2. at valley High School is the one I'm taking

    in English literature. It is taught by the
                            1   2   3   4

3. popular and able miss Rinehart, who has had many
    1   2   3   4

4. poems published in harper's and other excellent
    1   2   3   4

    1   2   3   4
5. magazines. she has even written a textbook

           1   2   3   4
6. on the subject which my friend, carol, in
    1   2   3   4
7. philadelphia says she is using in her studies.

60

DIRECTIONS: In the letter below, most lines have a number, such as 41, 42 or 43. If a punctuation mark is needed where the number is, mark the answer space for the
punctuation mark needed. If no punctuation is needed,
mark the N, which stands for None. Show either
apostrophes or single quotation marks in the fourth col-
umn. Only one answer should be given for each line.

MARKS OF PUNCTUATION (, : " ') N-None

LETTER

1821 Market Street

Dayton, Ohio

November 16, 1978

Mr. Walter H. Miller

Holiday Greeting Card Company

4129 Washington Avenue

New York 99$_{41}$ New York

Dear Mr. Miller_{42}

   Last week $_{43}$s shipment of Christmas cards arrived in

excellent condition. I think I already$_{44}$ have most of

them sold to friends, neighbors, and relatives. No$_{45}$ it

will not be necessary to send me another box. I think I

have made all the sale$_{46}$s I can for this year$_{47}$s holidays.

DIRECTIONS: Mark the number of the correct or better wo
in each sentence below.

1. If he had (^{1}went ^{2}gone) then, he would have been on
   time.

2. The word "Hurrah!" is (^{1}an interjection ^{2}a conjunctio

3. (^{1}Ins't ^{2}Aren't) the baskets filled with flowers?

4. My sister and (^{1}I ^{2}myself) will be glad to contribut

5. There are (^{1}eight ^{2}five) different parts of speech.

DIRECTIONS: For each statement given below that is a
complete sentence, mark YES; for each that is not, mark

1. Realizing that his capture was inevitable and being
   weak from lack of food to sustain his flight much
   longer, the escaped criminal, whose heart was beatin
   with fear.

2. The familiar way the plot was constructed gave us th
   impression we had seen the movie before.

3. Remembering the statement of our friends in our
   endeavor to overcome the difficulty.

4. The feeling that he had been there before haunted hi
   every step.

5. In the laundry room, with tubs and clothesbaskets pi
   full of clothes all ready to hang out as soon as the
   sun came out.

DIRECTIONS: Each line in this test contains four spelling words and the word, None. These words are numbered 1, 2, 3, 4, and the None is numbered 5. In some of the lines, one word is misspelled. In others, no word is misspelled. If there is a misspelled word, mark its number. If no word is misspelled, mark the 5.

	1	2	3	4	5
1.	Offense	reseipt	emphasis	deem	None
2.	approved	surprise	dreary	tractors	None
3.	muzeum	malice	comparative	principal	None
4.	successor	prinsiples	parole	recognition	None
5.	millinery	messenger	assignment	innacent	None
6.	federal	drama	bandit	proffesion	None
7.	apologize	herald	initeate	forfeit	None
8.	sensus	judgment	merit	liking	None
9.	mortal	postscript	differed	patroit	None
10.	wobbly	magnificent	eligible	fasilitate	None

63

SAMPLE QUESTIONS

Mathematics Skills Test

DIRECTIONS: There are 5 problems in this test. Following each problem there are five suggested answers. Work each problem in your head or on a piece of scratch paper. Then look at the five suggested answers and decide which one is correct.

1. A basketball team scored 14 points in the first quarter, 16 points in the second, 24 points in the third, and 14 points in the fourth. If they won by 14 points, how many points did the other team score?

    A. 14
    B. 40
    C. 54
    D. 68
    E. 82

2. A woman weighed 125 pounds. After she had gained 4½ pounds, lost 6 pounds, and gained 2½ pounds, how many pounds did she weigh?

    F. 124
    G. 125
    H. 126
    J. 137
    K. 138

3. How much more do 800 three-cent stamps cost than 150 two-cent stamps?

    A. $2.10
    B. $6.50
    C. $8.00
    D. $21.00
    E. $27.00

4. A boy saves $1.25 per week. How many weeks must he save before he can buy a $20 basketball?

    F. 6¼
    G. 12
    H. 15
    J. 16
    K. 25

5. If a girl knits half a scarf in 2 3/10 hours, how many hours should it take her to knit the whole scarf?

    A. 2 3/5   C. 4 3/10   E. 4 2/3
    B. 4 3/20   D. 4 3/5

COLLEGE LEVEL EXAMINATION PROGRAM
(CLEP)

HINTS FOR SCORING HIGH ON CLEP

It's really quite simple. Do things right...right from the beginning. Make successful methods a habit by practicing them on all the exercises. Before you're finished you will have invested a good deal of time. Make sure you get the largest dividends from this investment.

1. Be Confident. It is important to know that you are not expected to answer every question correctly on the CLEP Examinations. The questions have a range of difficulty and differentiate between several levels of skill. It's quite possible that an "A" student might answer no more than 60% of the questions correctly.

2. Skip Hard Questions and Go Back Later. There is a limit for each exam. You will not be expected to finish each exam. Even though you do not finish each one, you may still perform well in terms of your final score. However, it is important that you use your time well and pace yourself throughout the time allotted in order to answer as many questions as possible.

It is a good idea to make a mark on the question sheet next to all questions you cannot answer easily, and to go back to those questions later. First answer the questions you are sure about. Do not panic if you cannot answer a question. Go on and answer the questions you know. Usually the easier questions are presented at the beginning of the exam and the questions become gradually more difficult. However, all questions on this exam have equal weight in determining your score. no one question will receive more credit than any other regardless of difficulty. If you do skip ahead on the exam, be sure to skip ahead also on your answer sheet. A good technique is periodically to check the number of the question on the answer sheet with the number of the question on the test. You should do this every time you decide to skip a question. If you fail to skip over the corresponding answer blank for that question, all of your following answers will be wrong.

3. Guess If You Are Nearly Sure. Guessing is probably worthwhile if you have an intuition as to the correct answer or if you can eliminate one or more of the wrong options, and can thus make an "educated" guess. However, if you are entirely at a loss as to the correct answer, it may be best not to guess. A correction is made for guessing when the exam is scored. A percent-

age of wrong answers is subtracted from the number o
right answers. Therefore, it is sometimes better to
omit an answer than to guess.

4. Mark the Answer Sheet Clearly. When you take the
general or Subject Examinations, you will mark your
answers to the multiple-choice questions on a separa
answer sheet that will be given to you at the test
center. If you have not worked with an answer sheet
before, it is in your best interest to become famili
with the procedures involved. Remember, knowing the
correct answer is not enough! If you do not mark th
sheet correctly, so that it can be machine scored yo
will not get credit for your answers!

In addition to marking answers on the separate answe
sheet, you will also be asked to give your name and
other information, including your social security
number. (Remember, you must have your social securi
number for identification purposes.)

Read the directions carefully and follow them exactl
When you print your name in the boxes provided, writ
only one letter in each box. If your name is longer
than the number of boxes provided, omit the letters
that do not fit. Remember, you are writing for a
machine; it does not have judgment. It can only record the pencil marks you make on the answer sheet.

Use the answer sheet to record all your answers to
questions on both the General and Subject Examinatio
Each question, or item has five answer choices label
(A), (B), (C), (D), (E). You will be asked to choos
the letter for the alternative that best answers eac
question. Then you will be asked to mark your answe
by blackening the appropriate space on your answer
sheet. Be sure that each space you choose and black
with your pencil is completely blackened. If you
change your mind about an answer, or mark the wrong
space in error, you must erase the wrong answer.
Erase as thoroughly and neatly as possible. The mac
hine will "read" your answers in terms of spaces
blackened. Make sure that only one answer is clear
blackened.

5. Read Each Question Carefully. The questions on the
General Examinations are not designed to trick you
through misleading or ambiguous alternative choices.
On the other hand, they are not all direct questions
of factual information. Some are designed to elici

68

responses that reveal your ability to reason, or to interpret a fact or idea. It's up to you to read each question carefully so you know what is being asked. The exam authors have tried to make the questions clear. Do not go too far astray in looking for hidden meanings.

6. <u>Materials and Conduct At The Test Center</u>. You need to bring with you to the test center your Admission Form, your social security card and several No. 2 pencils. Arrive on time as you may not be admitted after testing has begun. Instructions for taking tests will be read to you by the test supervisor and time will be called when the test is over. If you have questions, you may ask them of the supervisors. Do not give or receive assistance while taking exams. If you do, you will be asked to turn in all test materials and told to leave the room. You will not be permitted to return and your tests will not be scored. The College Board also reserves the right to cancel your score at any time it there is any reason to question its accuracy. However, before exercising its right to cancel a score, the Board will offer the student a chance to take the test again at no additional fee. (2: 23-24)

REFERENCES

REFERENCES

1. California Language Test, Devised by Ernest W. Tiegs
   and Willis W. Clark, 1957 Edition, published by
   California Testing Bureau.

2. College Level Examination Program by David R. Turner,
   M.S. in Education, Arco Publishing Company, Inc.,
   New York, New York, 1977.

3. Cooperative English Tests, Cooperative Test Division,
   Educational Testing Service, 1960.

4. Cooperative School and College Ability Tests, 1955,
   Educational Testing Service, Princeton, New Jer-
   sey.

5. Corbin, Charles B., et al. Concepts for Physical
   Education, Second Edition, William C. Brown,
   Publishing Company, Dubuque, Iowa, 1974.

6. Iowa Silent Reading Tests, New Edition, by
   H. A. Greens, Director, Bureau of Educational
   Research and Service, University of Iowa;
   A. M. Jorgenson, President, University of
   Connecticut and V. H. Kelley, University Appoint-
   ment Office, University of Arizona, Tucson,
   Arizona.

7. Mathematics Skills Test, Norfolk State College,
   Norfolk, Virginia, 1978.

8. Parent's Guide to Understanding Tests, McGraw-Hill
   Publishing Company, Monterey, California, 1976.

9. Scholastic Aptitude Test, by David R. Turner, M.S. in
   Education, Arco Publishing Company, Inc., New
   York, New York, 1977.

10. Survey of Study Habits and Attitudes, Brown-Holtzman,
    1965, The Psychological Corporation, 304 East 45th
    Street, New York, New York, 10017.

11. Testing: Its Place in Education Today, Chauncey and
    Dobbin, Harper and Row Publishing Company, 1963.

APPENDIX

TEST HIM! TEST HIM! THUS SAYETH THE LORD

By R. R. Alford, Ph. D.

Erving Goffman, in his book, **Stigma**, speaks of what he terms "social identity" to describe how a society establish- ed a means of categorizing persons and the set of attribut- es felt to be ordinary and natural for members of each of these categories. He goes on to say "When a stranger comes into our presence, then, first appearances are likely to enable us to anticipate his category and attributes." In this manner, an individual and a group of individuals is ascribed a social identity. Now, when an individual appears to those who hold the power of social judgment to possess attributes that make him different from others in the category of persons available for him to be, and of a less desirable kind he is, according to Goffman, ". . .thus reduced in our minds from a whole and usual person to a tainted, discounted one. Such an attribute is a stigma, especailly when its discrediting effect is very extensive."

The stigma that has been leveled against people of African descent in America provides me with justification for opening my presentation with Goffman's description of the stigmatization process. Black people are stigmatized by what Dr. Francis G. Welsing of Howard University calls the "only functional racism in the known universe"--white supremacy. Let us never forget that Black people were brought to America as chattels --- movable property of white folks. The stigmatization began with the first encounter with Africans by whites, who because of their conquering chauvinism, viewed differences in values, religion, customs, and skin color as inferior. The result was a need felt by whites to Christianize and humanize the "dark-skinned savages". This was the beginnings of the great Diaspora and subsequently the beginnings of African history in America.

I have been asked many times to defend the existence of cultural biases in psychological testing. In view of what we all know of American history, my defense states that Black people in this country have been stigmatized by racism, racism is institutionalized, education is an insti- tution, psychological testing is symbiotically related to education and I rest my case. Unless it is necessary for me to enter a discourse on the extent to which racism is institutionalized in America.

One of my most admired colleagues, Dr. Robert L. Williams of Washington University in

St. Louis, recently wrote that "universities have launche
research into various aspects of the 'black problem.' Th
white belief system has determined their selection of bla
as a problem, how they should be studied, and what the
solutions shall be." As a matter of fact, I am penning
this manuscript for the very same reasons Dr. Williams ha
outlined--to present an argument on a question to which t
answer is known by most of the persons that will read thi
article. Dr. Williams has stated further in reference to
what he has termed "scientific racism" that: "the black-
white IQ controversy presents

> an analogus situation. When a people is labeled
> consistently as being of low-intellect or simple-
> minded, the respect among the general populace for
> their rights of life can and will erode to nothing.
> It has happened here. The Black Community has
> become the white researcher's hunting ground,
> the ideal experimental laboratory."

Dr. Williams does not stop here, however, he goes on to
question any research which stems from an attempt to iso
differences between groups of human beings as efforts at
dehumanization. And he is not alone in the area, psycho
gist Charles Thomas says research of this type is based
"...a belief that Black people are similar enough to whi
people to permit measurement by common instruments, and
different enough from white people to justify scientific
research into the causes of the differences."

My position is that psychological tests reveal noth
more than a score and under no circumstances should be us
as indices of intelligence. Peter Koening writing in
Psychology Today accurately assesses that the purpose of
psychology testing is ".... to measure differences betwe
individuals." Koening also points out that psychologica
testing has replaced the old credentiality system wherei
the right family and Ivy League diploma served as the st
dard governing over who is going to judge whom. And sin
1964, when the clause added to the 1964 Civil Rights Act
Senator Tower of Texas established that it shall not be

> "... unlawful employment practice for an
> employer to give and to act upon the results
> of any professionally developed ability test,
> provided that such test, its administration
> or action upon the results, is not designed,
> intended or used to discriminate because of
> race, color, religion, sex or national origin."

74

It has become illegal for an employer to turn an individual down for a job because he is Black, Chicano, Puerto Rican, West Indian, Oriental, Apache, but is quite all right to turn him down if he scored low on an intelligence test.

What in fact do the test measure? According to Louis L. Knowles and Kenneth Prewitt in Institutional Racism in America, the daughters of well-to-do white city dwellers show up best of all on intelligence tests and it should surprise no one that they do because it happens to be that the tests themselves are prepared by well-to-do white city dwellers. Knowles and Prewitt also convey that the "form and language and the conditions under which they (IQ test) are given cannot fail to be products of a culture ...In fact, the very practice of using a pencil and paper test to measure intelligence is itself a factor that will culturally bias the examination."

Though I have spoken primarily about the inherent cultural biases of IQ testing against Black people, the point made by Knowles and Prewitt has implications for any group of people not part of Middle America. Intelligence tests are comparisons, scores on such test compare the individual to a group of individuals. If the group to which scores are compared is predominantly white, middle-class, urban dwellers, then poor, rural dwellers of any race who have not had the same experiences and are not subject to comparison. As educators, our concern must be quality education for all. [P.L. 94-142]

We have been guilty of using IQ tests to measure the amount and intensity of education that we will disseminate to students. The brighter students are expected to do well and we help them to do well, the less bright students are expected to fail and we help them to fail. But how have we differentiated the bright from the less bright. We have, in effect, said those who rate the closest in similarity to the daughters of white-middle class-urban dwellers are our prizes, those who do not are our misfortune. Dr. Robert L. Greene points out in an article entitled "The Awesome Danger of 'Intelligence' Tests" that in regard to the middle-income Anglo-Saxon, it is the culture of this group -- their expectations, beliefs and language-- (which) has dominated American life and education. Success in public schools has been judged on how well a child understands and masters this culture." Intelligence tests have been based on a white, middle income view of intelligence.

I do not advocate the total elimination of testing.
do advocate the total elimination of use of tests as a
means of measuring intellignece and the quality of education a child will receive. We know that many tests are
biased, but for that matter so are the public schools
themselves, in favor of white middle America. Right now,
the institutionalization of these biases is quite firmly
entrenched in the public schools and it is going to take
more than an academic discussion to alter that. But we,
as academicians, can be aware of test biases and begin to
educate all children -- not just those whom the texts
say possess the greatest potential for becoming Middle-
Americans.

ANSWERS

PART I (SCAT)

1. E
2. J
3. B
4. J
5. A

PART II (SCAT)

1. A
2. H
3. A
4. H
5. B

PART III (SCAT)

1. B
2. F
3. D
4. H
5. E

Iowa Silent Reading Test (Page 47)

1. 3
2. 2
3. 1

Page 48

1. 2
2. 4
3. 6
4. 7
5. 10

Page 49

1. 4
2. 1
3. 7
4. 6
5. 10
6. 13

Answers (cont'd)

Page 50

1. 3.
2. 4
3. 2
4. 1
5. 1

Page 50

1. Yes
2. Yes
3. No
4. No
5. No
6. Yes

Page 51

A. 2
B. 1
C. 2

Page 52

1. 3
2. 1
3. 5

Page 52

1. 2
2. 4
3. 2
4. 1
5. 3

Page 54

1. D
2. G
3. A
4. H
5. A

Page 55

1. A
2. O
3. B
4. E
5. A

Page 58

1. R
2. A
3. R
4. R
5. A
6. R
7. A
8. R
9. R
10. R

Page 60

1. N
2. 2
3. 1
4. 3
5. 2
6. 4
7. 1

Page 61

1. ,
2. :
3. '
4. N
5. ,
6. N
7. '

Page 62

1. 2
2. 1
3. 2
4. 1
5. 1

Answers cont'd.)

Page 62

1. No
2. Yes
3. No
4. Yes
5. No

Page 63

1. 2
2. 5
3. 1
4. 2
5. 4
6. 4
7. 3
8. 1
9. 5
10. 4

Page 64

1. C
2. H
3. D
4. J
5. D